INVEST IN THE FUTURE

Diane Lindsey Reeves

21st Century Junior Library

Published in the United States of America by:

CHERRY LAKE PRESS
2395 South Huron Parkway, Suite 200, Ann Arbor, Michigan 48104
www.cherrylakepress.com

Reading Adviser: Beth Walker Gambro, MS, Ed., Reading Consultant, Yorkville, IL

Photo Credits: © Studio Romantic/Shutterstock, cover; © Rido/Shutterstock, 5; © Viktoriia Hnatiuk/Shutterstock, 6; © Wara1982/Shutterstock, 7; © Drazen Zigic/shutterstock, 8–9; © Andrey_Popov/Shutterstock, 10–11; © Adha Ghazali/Shutterstock, 13; © jd8/Shutterstock, 14; © PeopleImages.com - Yuri A/Shutterstock, 16; © Suphakant/Shutterstock, 19

Copyright © 2026 by Cherry Lake Publishing Group
All rights reserved. No part of this book may be reproduced or utilized in any form or by any means without written permission from the publisher.

Cherry Lake Press is an imprint of Cherry Lake Publishing Group.

Library of Congress Cataloging-in-Publication Data has been filed and is available at catalog.loc.gov.

Cherry Lake Publishing Group would like to acknowledge the work of the Partnership for 21st Century Learning, a Network of Battelle for Kids. Please visit Battelle for Kids online for more information.

Printed in the United States of America

Note from publisher: Websites change regularly, and their future contents are outside of our control. Supervise children when conducting any recommended online searches for extended learning opportunities.

CONTENTS

Chapter 1: Discover the Investing in the Future Career Cluster — 4

Chapter 2: Explore Investing in the Future Careers — 10

Chapter 3: Is Investing in the Future in Your Future? — 17

Activity — 21
Glossary — 22
Find Out More — 23
Index — 24
About the Author — 24

DISCOVER THE INVESTING IN THE FUTURE CAREER CLUSTER

Everyone needs money. It pays for basic needs like food and shelter. Money pays for schools and health care. It funds businesses. It funds governments. Money can help people retire when they get older. This all takes planning.

Want to help people grow and manage their wealth? This may be the career cluster for you!

The Investing in the Future cluster from the National Career Clusters® Framework is all about money. Some careers focus on managing it. Some focus on saving it. Others focus on protecting or investing it. These careers help people take good care of money.

Investing in the Future careers require a lot of math, like analyzing data. Keep practicing!

Look!

Did you know that salt and cacao beans were once used as money? With an adult, look online to learn about the history of money. What interesting types of currency can you find?

You must be good at math to do many of these careers. Sometimes a college degree is needed. These careers may take special training or experience. People with these careers mostly work in offices.

Real estate agents are part of this cluster. They work hard to help people rent or buy homes.

Let's explore the five Investing in the Future career areas:

- Accounting
- Banking
- Insurance
- **Investments**
- Real Estate

Create!

Keep track of the money you earn and spend. You may earn money from gifts. You may earn it from doing chores. You spend it on things you want or need. Use these numbers to make a budget. Be sure to save some money. Do your numbers add up?

EXPLORE INVESTING IN THE FUTURE CAREERS

The average American earns 1.7 million dollars in their life. That's a lot of money! But they need to make it last. Investing in the Future careers help people use money wisely.

Accounting is a way to keep track of money. It records money earned and spent. It does this for people and businesses. Bookkeepers keep track of day-to-day spending. They keep track of income. They pay bills.

Are you organized? Accountants always need to know where to find important financial records. They need to make sure bills get paid on time. Could accounting be right for you?

Accountants organize money data. This is used to make choices about money. **Forensic** accountants help solve crimes. These crimes have to do with money.

Banking careers manage money. Bankers give people advice about money. They do the same for businesses. They manage loans.

Insurance protects people from risks. It does the same for businesses. Insurance agents sell insurance plans.

Actuaries use **statistics**. This type of math predicts risks. A risk is something that could hurt a company. Risks range from natural disasters to lawsuits.

Insurance protects people and things they own. It helps pay for loss or injury when they happen.

Money can grow over time through investments.

Investments help money grow into more money. **Bonds** and **stocks** are examples. People buy these as investments. Bonds and stocks will both usually help people earn money over time. Financial planners give people advice about investments. Stockbrokers buy and sell stocks.

Real estate is buildings and land that people own. Real estate agents help people buy and sell homes. They do the same for other property. Mortgage brokers help people get loans. These loans help people buy real estate.

Make a Guess!

Imagine you put $500 in a bank account. This account earns 5 percent interest each year. Guess how much the account would grow in 10 years. Ask an adult to help you use an online compound interest calculator. This program will help you figure it out.

If you enjoy working with numbers, a career in finance may be for you.

IS INVESTING IN THE FUTURE IN YOUR FUTURE?

Do you like math and working with numbers? Are you interested in money? If your answer is yes, that's your first clue! Investing in the Future careers might be right for you.

There is no rush! You have time. But it can be fun to check out the options. Figure out what you like to do. Think of what you want to know more about.

These clues will help narrow down your choices. Learn about yourself and explore different careers. These are good ways to be a career-ready kid.

You can experiment with career ideas, too. Ask an adult to help you talk to someone with a career that interests you. An adult can help you visit places where these people work. Think about what the work is like. Imagine the kinds of problems you can solve.

Being a career-ready kid **motivates** you to do your best work now. You can build a bridge from learning in school to preparing for your future career.

Think!

Which of the areas in this career cluster interests you most? Is it accounting or banking? Can you see yourself as a financial advisor? Would investments be a good choice? Or would you rather work with insurance or real estate?

There are so many careers that work with money! You have plenty of time to decide if one of them will be a good fit for you.

INVESTIGATE INVESTING IN THE FUTURE CAREERS

Real Estate
- appraiser
- loan processor
- mortgage broker
- property manager
- purchasing agent

Analyzing & Strategizing
- budget analyst
- financial planner
- stockbroker

Accounting
- accountant
- forensic accountant

INVEST IN THE FUTURE

Insurance
- actuary
- claims analyst
- insurance adjuster
- insurance agent
- insurance investigator

Management
- banker
- bank manager
- business manager
- chief financial officer
- comptroller

ACTIVITY

Practice managing your money! Think about how you get money. Do you do chores? Do you earn an allowance? Do you have another way? Keep track of how much money you earn.

- Think through things you want to spend money on. Do you want to buy a new video game? Do you want to get a new bike? Do you want to buy a gift for a friend? How much will these things cost?

- Make a plan to save for your goals. Example: If you earn $10 each week, how many weeks would it take to buy a bike that costs $120?

Ask Questions!

The way people pay their bills has changed over time. They used to go to banks, write checks, or pay in cash. Now they use ATMs, debit cards, and apps. How do you think people in the future will pay their bills?

GLOSSARY

actuaries (AK-chuh-wer-eez) people who use math to figure out how much insurance should cost to cover for different risks

bonds (BAHNDZ) loans made by investors to businesses and governments; over time, investors receive their money back with interest

budget (BUH-juht) a plan for money that helps people or businesses spend and save the money they earn in the ways that they want or need

cacao beans (kuh-KOW BEENZ) beans that are roasted and ground up to make cocoa powder

compound interest (KAHM-pownd IN-tuh-ruhst) interest paid on interest in a savings account or investment

currency (KUHR-uhn-see) the type of money used in a country

forensic (fuh-REN-sik) describing when scientific knowledge is used to solve legal problems

interest (IN-tuh-ruhst) a fee paid for borrowing money or the money earned on investments

investments (in-VEST-muhnts) money spent in a way to help it grow; common investments include stocks, bonds, and real estate

motivates (MOH-tuh-vayts) provides a person with a reason for taking action

statistics (stuh-TIH-stiks) type of math that helps people figure out the chance of something happening

stocks (STAHKS) shares in a public business that investors buy and sell

FIND OUT MORE

Books

Fitzpatrick, Kalpana. *Get to Know Money.* New York, NY: DK Children, 2022.

Hobson, Mellody. *Priceless Facts About Money.* Somerville, MA: Candlewick, 2024.

Marsico, Katie. *Understanding Investing.* Ann Arbor, MI: Cherry Lake Publishing, 2025.

Reeves, Diane Lindsey. *Finance: Exploring Career Pathways.* Ann Arbor, MI: Cherry Lake Publishing, 2018.

Websites

Explore these online resources with an adult.

Coin Classroom: U.S. Mint for Kids

Federal Deposit Insurance Corporation (FDIC): Money Smart News for Kids

INDEX

accounting careers, 9, 10–12, 20
activities, 21
actuaries, 12, 21

banking careers, 9, 12, 20
bill paying, 21
bonds, 14
bookkeepers, 10
budgeting, 9, 20–21

career choices, 9, 17–20
career clusters, 4–6, 18
compound interest, 15
currency, 7

earnings, 10, 21
education paths, 7, 18

forensic accounting, 12

insurance careers, 9, 12–13, 20
interest, 15
interests, 9, 17–20
investing careers, 4–6, 9, 12, 14, 20

learning and training, 7, 18

math skills, 6–7, 12, 16–17
money management careers, 4–6, 9, 12, 14, 20
money, purpose of, 4

real estate careers, 8–9, 15, 18, 20
risk management, 12–13

saving money, 6, 9, 15, 21
statistics, 12
stocks, 14

ABOUT THE AUTHOR

Diane Lindsey Reeves writes books to help students of all ages find bright futures. She lives in North Carolina with her husband and a big kooky dog named Honey. She has four of the best grandkids in the world.